Dinosaur Publications

Making a Car

by Althea

illustrated by Timothy Hunkin

Published by Dinosaur Publications Ltd Over Cambridge England

ISBN 85122/074/6

First the car must be designed. Men work at drawing boards to decide the best shape for the body.

Other men try out the best way
to make the engine.
They must make a quiet engine
and be careful that it will
not make smelly smoke.

The designers make a wooden model
for the other factory men to see.
Then they make one car
and fit an engine into it.
They drive it on the road
to make sure it works properly.

OIL
FUEL

They can now start making
lots more cars just like it.
Cars are usually made
in very big factories
and their parts are made
by great big machines.

The car is moved along
from one worker to another.
They each fix on a part of the car,
until it comes out finished
at the other end.

But the car in our book
is made partly by machines
and partly with hand tools.

Flat pieces of metal are cut out
and pressed into shape
to make the bonnet and the boot
and the other parts of the car.

Then they make the chassis which is the underneath part.

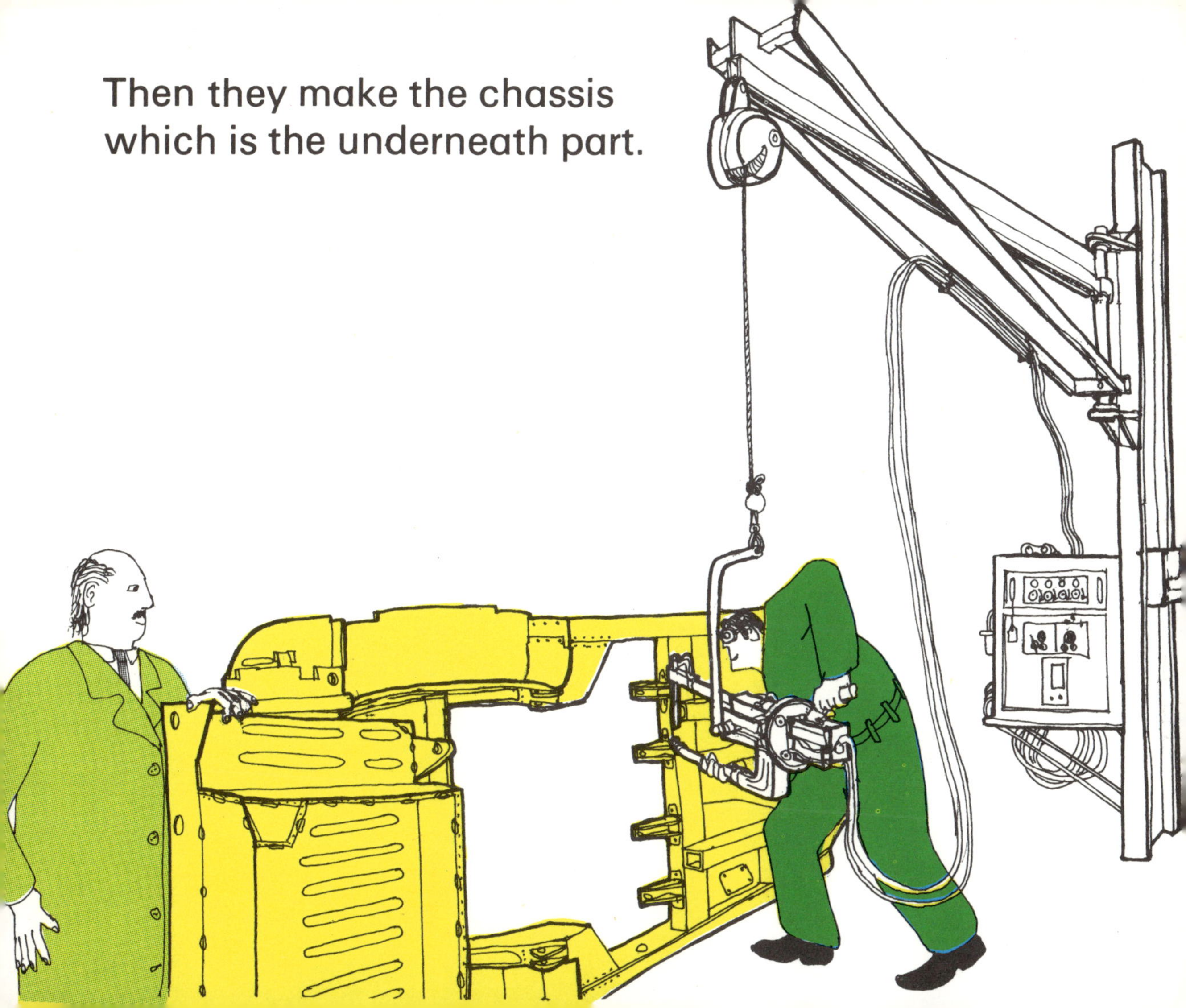

Next, the body parts are all
fixed onto the chassis
by welding them together
with hot melted metal.

The car is sprayed with
a special dull paint
which stops it going rusty.

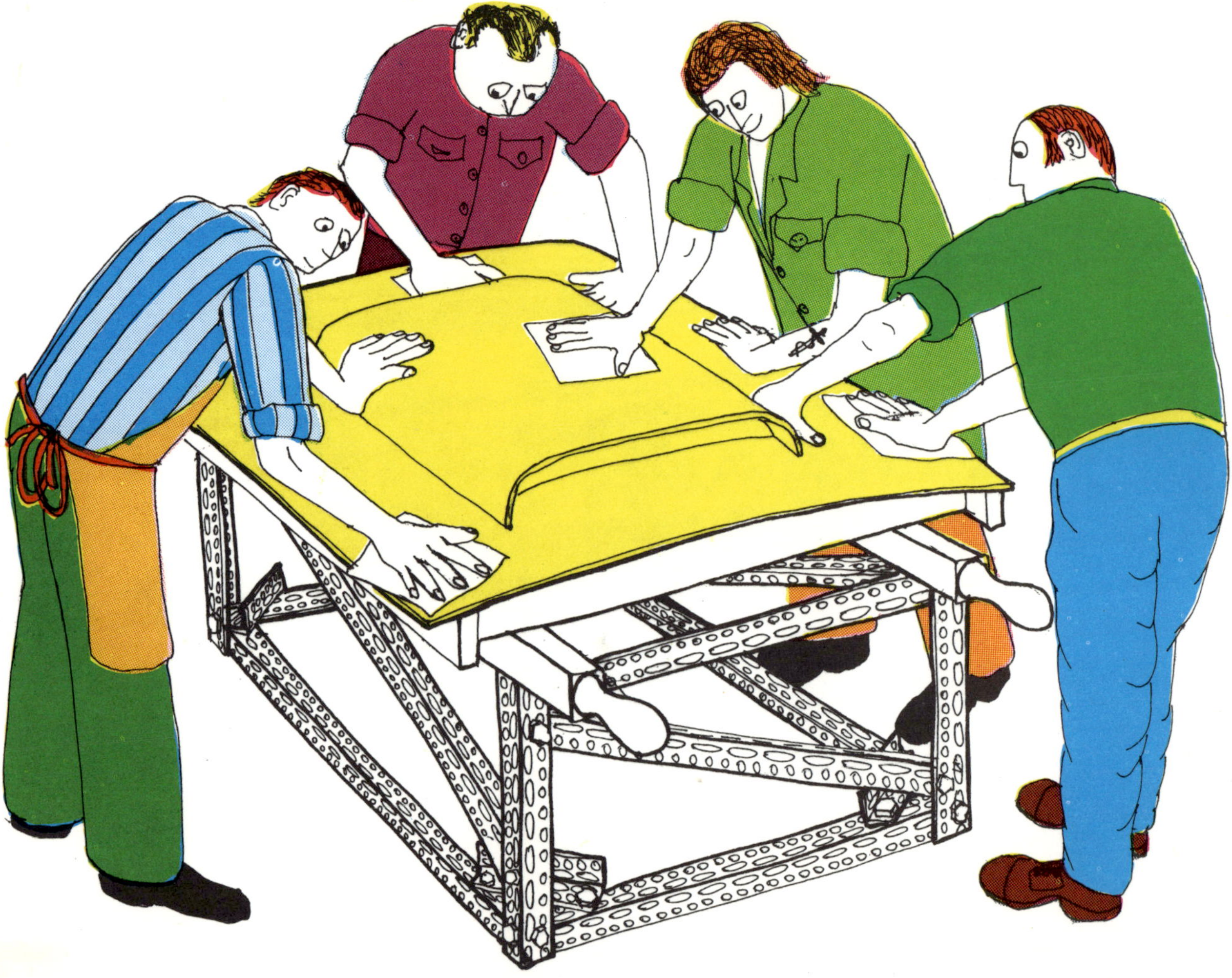

Then it is smoothed down and
painted a bright shiny colour.
Now the car goes into an oven
to bake on the paint
and make it very hard.

The wheels are put on next
so the car can be pushed along.
Then they can work on it
in different parts of the factory.

The lamps and windows are fitted.
Inside, the dials and knobs are fixed.

All the parts of the engine
are carefully made
and fixed tightly together.
Then the whole engine
is bolted onto the chassis.

In another part of the factory,
leather is being cut up
and sewn to make the seats.
With very clean hands
they are gently fitted
into the car.

At last the car is finished.
But before it leaves the factory
it is carefully tested to make sure
everything works properly.

Some cars are collected
by their new owners
from the factory.

Others are carried away
by car transporters
for garages to sell.